HOW I HEALED MYSELF OF CHRONIC PAIN AFTER 17 YEARS

by
Pirkko Monds

(And Lost 40 Kilograms in the Process)

Copyright © 2022 (Pirkko Monds)
All rights reserved worldwide.

No part of this publication may be reproduced or transmitted in any form or by any means, electronic or mechanical, including photocopy, recording, or any information storage and retrieval system, without permission in writing from the author.

Publisher: Inspiring Publishers,
P.O. Box 159, Calwell, ACT Australia 2905
Email: publishaspg@gmail.com
http://www.inspiringpublishers.com

 A catalogue record for this book is available from the National Library of Australia

National Library of Australia The Prepublication Data Service

Author: Pirkko Monds
Title: How I Healed Myself of Chronic Pain After 17 Years
Genre: Non-fiction

Print ISBN: 978-1-922792-97-6
eBook ISBN: 978-1-922792-98-3

SINCERE THANKS TO:

Robert, my husband and partner of 50 years. Robert and I have been through a lot together. He has been my carer for many years and has loved and supported me through my darkest moments. Thank you, Robert, for everything you have seen me through.

Hannele, our oldest daughter, a mental health nurse and naturopath, thank you Hannele for your continuous support and love. You were always ready to listen to all I was going through and embrace with compassion whatever trauma I needed to discuss. Thank you Hannele for your guidance and the advice you gave me, which is appreciated forever.

Shireen, our youngest daughter, who always had positive practical ways of supporting my journey. When moving Shireen was there to help me pack and sort out my pantry and household items when I didn't have the energy to even make an intelligent decision about where everything was to go. When in hospital Shireen would always arrive with delicious things to eat, as she is such a great cook. Thank you, Shireen, for your love and support.

My Gift to Humanity

*Although the world is full of suffering,
it is also full of the overcoming of it.
- Helen Keller*

REFERENCES

BREAKING THE HABIT OF BEING YOURSELF by Dr Joe Dispenza

BECOMING SUPERNATURAL by Dr Joe Dispenza

YOU ARE THE PLACEBO by Dr Joe Dispenza

EVOLVE YOUR BRAIN by Dr Joe Dispenza

THE BIOLOGY OF BELIEF by Bruce Lipton, Ph.D.

THE SPONTANEOUS HEALING OF BELIEF by Gregg Braden

THE WISDOM CODES by Gregg Braden

TAPPING THE HEALER WITHIN by Rodger J. Callahan, Ph.D.

Dr Joe Dispenza's ONLINE INTENSIVE COURSE

Many You Tube videos on Dr Joe Dispenza Meditations

And lectures and testimonials from all over the world.

TABLE OF CONTENTS

INTRODUCTION 1
MY BACKGROUND 3
HOW DISEASE SETS IN 7
MY WORKING LIFE 9
FROM WORKING LIFE TO ILLNESS 11
LIFE GETS EVEN HARDER 15
I DESCEND INTO A DARK SPACE 18
A LIGHT SHINES IN THE DISTANCE 23
WE LOOK FOR A PERMANENT BASE 26
MY REAL EDUCATION BEGINS 28
THE KETOGENIC DIET 30
SHOPPING & GETTING STARTED 32
STEPS WHICH I TOOK 34
REPLACING THE OLD FAMILIAR FOODS
WITH HEALTHIER OPTIONS 36
WHY DOES THE KETOGENIC DIET HELP YOU
LOSE WEIGHT? 37
INTERMITTENT FASTING 39
EXERCISE 41

DR JOE DISPENZA COMES INTO MY LIFE 43
WHOLE FOOD PLANT BASED DIET 50
2022 IS HERE NOW 56
CONCLUSION 61
VISUALS 65

Reviews

I have known Pirkko since we started at Sydney Kindergarten Teachers College in 1973. We always stayed in touch and then undertook our momentous task together setting up Millthorpe Children's Garden, a Steiner inspired childcare centre in 2005.

Pirkko is a truly inspired person, she gives all her energy and commitment to whatever she is creating. Her intentions are strong and pure. Her determination and belief in divine energy has carried her through a myriad of dark spaces for a very long time.

I have been with her during many of these times and now when I see her, a completely changed person in so many ways, I see a miracle, a truly well-deserved miracle.

Judith Boag

This book is truly an inspiration. It chronicles the remarkable life of Pirkko, from her native Finland to her arrival in rural Australia. Speaking no English when she arrived in Australia, she and her family, like so many others, came with the hope of a better life. Many migrant families experienced hardships, and what followed for Pirkko during her early years were physical illnesses and many traumas. But it was her indomitable spirit and energy that endeared her to so many school friends, one of whom is Robert, her partner of 50 years, and another was my beloved wife, Pam, who passed away in 2013. Coincidentally, both Pam and Pirkko were diagnosed with different forms of cancer at around the same time. It was a devastating time for all.

I am glad Pirkko has written this book. A book to tell her story. A book I can vouch for, as since coming to know Pirkko after meeting my wife Pam, back in 1981, I have witnessed everything Pirkko has reported in this book. It is true, and it is inspirational. Her struggles and transformation from illness to health, through perseverance and openness to new ideas, is a lesson for us all.

Dr David Harding

INTRODUCTION

My name is Pirkko Monds. I am writing my story to help others out there who have gone through similar experiences to me. I know from statistics, that one in five people over the age of 45 suffer with some sort of persistent or ongoing pain. I am not a doctor or medically trained, so the story I relay is NOT medical advice. It is simply my story of how pain began within my body at the age of forty-nine. I go through all the steps I took with doctors, specialists, pain clinics and different therapists to try and regain back my health.

The story I am about to give you in the pages to follow, spans at least two decades, even though only recognising now, that many of the signs of potential illness were with me many decades prior to this. At the time earlier on in my life, I didn't conceptualise the idea that many of the symptoms I was experiencing could in any way lead to illness or disease down the track.

The last two decades have been a massive learning process. Not only have I come to know we have access to so much information online, but I have learnt to open my mind to the possibility of embracing 'healing' from many different people and places around me. I have come to realise the importance of sifting through everything you may be presented with, and then using your God-given discerning intelligence to take in what resonates with you, while putting the rest aside. This includes the advice of well-meaning family and friends. We all have different ways of approaching anything and learning to respect another's personal journey is one of my biggest lessons.

MY BACKGROUND

I am a Finnish born Australian, having migrated, as a five- year-old, in 1959 with my family. This was at a time, when Australia was welcoming European migrants to come to the 'Land of Opportunity' to take up the many jobs needed in the "Land Down Under".

I went to school not speaking a word of English, but like most children at that age was able to learn to communicate within months. As a child I was told, I was emotional, sensitive and highly strung. I would cry very easily, get upset very easily and carry worries from wherever they came from. When I would question my mother about this asking 'why does everything have to be so hard?', she would say 'we are meant to suffer', and this was believed by many in that era.

This stuck with me all throughout my life. I do not blame anyone for anything I have gone through, as I believe we choose these experiences prior to our incarnation to learn what we need to learn from our human earthly experience. Because I went through many traumatic incidences throughout early childhood, primary school years, as well as a teenager, I always felt I was sensitive and perceived everything around me to be bad or scary or negative. This is part of your childhood programming from the environment your live in, and moulds you into the adult you become. It is quite true that each individual human being filters through the lens of their own experience, some personalities take things harder than others, but traumas also accumulate.

If a child has no way of navigating through experiences or events that impact them mentally, emotionally, and physically, these energies can become stuck in the body and cause disease down the track.

At the age of 11, I was at the dentist, and he had just given me a needle to deaden the pain as he was about to drill. My heart started racing in my chest and I passed out. After coming to consciousness, the dentist asked about what I felt. I told him I could feel my heart going very fast and I thought it would burst out of my chest. It was then that I learned of my first medical allergy to the substance we know of as adrenalin. I was told by the dentist that my body is too highly strung to handle adrenalin in the needle they routinely give in a local anaesthetic. This allergy has remained with me to this day, having to routinely explain to all dentists not to use adrenalin, and any doctor who may be using a local anaesthetic to do any routine procedure. I ignored this in 2012 just before I was diagnosed with breast cancer during a biopsy, and the same thing happened, my heart raced, and I ended up passing out and was sent to emergency.

During my early childhood years in Finland, I had asthma, and when I came to Australia, I grew out of it by about age nine. Being Finnish the *sauna,* which was our bathroom, was heated up regularly. I fainted in the sauna, if I got too much of the hot steam, and this made me very wary of going into a very hot sauna from then on. I do not remember what age this started, but I knew to be very conscious of it.

At age 12 I got rheumatic fever, which seemed to go on forever. I missed a lot of school, my mother was very worried about me, and it left me very weak and unable to do the normal things which a twelve- year- old does. I remember laying delirious on the bed as my fingers turned achy and arthritic, and my mother had to feed me. The arthritis remained with me from then on, plus a heart murmur. Whatever happened inside my body after that I really cannot explain in any scientific terms. I often felt weak and the feeling of not having enough energy. At age 14 I was put onto penicillin for the rheumatic fever. I had no idea how that would have helped, but I had to remain on this medication for five years. There was always this strange kind of agitation inside me, which I couldn't explain. This became worse over time, and I would often feel like passing out.

I pressed on through life, trying hard at my school and doing reasonably well. I remember during the rheumatic fever my mother was concerned that I would never be able to take on a job where I was on my feet. It was decided from that moment, that I aspire to become a secretary, so I could at least work sitting down. After completing year 10 in 1970, I was awarded a scholarship to do secretarial studies at the Technical College in Sydney. I felt my life path was planned out before me. Not long after the results of the School Certificate came out, we had one of the teachers from the high school at our door ready to speak to my parents. I had done better in the School Certificate than I could ever have imagined. I had come 6th out of 120 students. That gave me a good feeling about myself, having lacked confidence in my abilities for a long time. I told my parents that they were recommending that I return and complete high school and I could probably go to university, although at the time I had no desire to do so, and quite frankly found school a completely tedious task, which only served one agenda, and that was to get another piece of paper so you could get a better job, so you could make more money, so you could get ahead like everyone else, so you could be like everyone else. This was the way I viewed the whole education concept as an adult, although I felt, in my teens, I needed to aspire to "make something of myself". As a sixteen-year-old trying to make a decision about my future, the only things I truly enjoyed doing were singing, dancing and cooking. I did belong to the school choir, but when I wanted to do home science, it was not a matriculation subject, so my passion was put aside.

After much soul- searching I went back to school. I did find all of it a lot of hard work and very stressful. My one saving grace during year 12 was that I began going out with a boy from the same class of year12, and Robert and I are still together now, 50 years later. When I did get into most of the universities and teacher's colleges, I decided that all I really wanted to do was sing and tell stories to young children. Singing was very much encouraged in the family by both parents and that to me was very enjoyable. To this day I know many songs in Finnish and sing them to keep up my mother tongue. I chose to become a preschool teacher and started at Waverley Kindergarten Teachers College in 1973.

Robert and I were married in 1976, and had two daughters, the first in 1982 and the second in 1985.

HOW DISEASE SETS IN

We are all wise in hindsight. I never recognised what was going on in my body. From the time I could remember I have been passing out from one thing or another. If I was worried about something, which was often, if I didn't eat regularly, if I had too much sugar, if I was too hot, if I did too much exercise, or if I could perceive fear or anger in my environment. The list goes on and on. I realised at the age of 66, when I began my self-healing journey that I had spent most of my life in a continual state of 'fight or flight', which activates cortisol and adrenalin, 'in case you are being pursued by a sabre- toothed tiger.' This was an evolutionary mechanism in our system to keep ourselves safe. Over time, I knew that this agitation inside my body, could be turned on through thought alone, but I had no idea about the damage I was doing to my own health. It was the reason I always felt this strange nervous reaction within my body which I could not explain or control. I would often say to Robert 'I feel funny', not knowing what this agitation was. Many years after experiencing this I can now easily call it 'anxiety'.

One doctor whom Robert worked for, was with me when I passed out, and he was the first to try and explain what I was going through. I was 26 at the time, and he said I had an overactive sympathetic nervous system. I didn't really understand what that meant, and no solution was given to me on how to solve this problem.

During our married life, we lived on some very isolated properties. We had no children at that time, and I was studying by correspondence to be a primary school teacher. I was interested in cooking and nutrition and began baking healthy bread and improving our diet as much as I knew how. Even though this probably helped to some degree, the agitation inside me never left. I pushed through life the best I knew how, not ever knowing that being tired, lacking sleep, worrying about everything and anything, always feeling inadequate or feeling I needed to do more in life and please everyone around me, was continually down grading me for disease. Along the way I did try affirmations and other techniques, but nothing ever got to the core of the problem.

MY WORKING LIFE

I took on many different teaching jobs during my working life in various regional towns while Robert managed large properties with thousands of sheep, cattle or whatever else the farm owner had. I became qualified in primary school teaching to make it easier to get work. My favourite primary schools were the one or two teacher schools. I took on short term jobs as a casual teacher and they were very enjoyable. Once I went to work in the larger schools, I suffered a lot with stress because of the pressure from around me to perform a certain way. In one of these positions, I fainted in front of the children and was very close to losing my job. I was a casual primary school teacher for 16 years.

Since I had done so much training, I was always able to obtain senior preschool positions and I knew deep down that I was very good at doing this type of work. I loved singing, and that went down very well with all the children I had ever come across. I also loved making up songs and stories and actions poems. I knew how to encourage the learning process in young children in a totally fun way.

During my working life I was also very interested in any kind of spiritual education I could acquire. I would do different short workshops that brought me great happiness and connected me with like- minded people. While the children were still very young, Robert's back began to get very tight and achy. He had lots of work done on his back by acupuncturists and chiropractors which helped a little, but nothing helped long term. When his doctor began talking about operating and just fusing all his vertebra, we began thinking outside the square. Afterall he was only 36, and we couldn't believe they would even jump straight into something so drastic. I heard about a course called Reiki. It sounded, very much, out of mainstream medical health. Being opened minded I was prepared to go and do the course, which might help him heal. It took about three weeks before I felt the energy flowing through me and he began to feel the benefits of the Reiki energy. I began to soften his muscles with this energy, and he got some relief. We soon began to realise that if I could massage those muscles which had been warmed and softened with Reiki, then he may even get more relief. So again, I went and did a second course, a Certificate in Remedial Massage and finally a Diploma. From this treatment, every day, Robert made a full recovery, and was back working and playing tennis, pain free, within nine months. He was so thankful for his recovery that he himself did all the courses I had completed, so we would be able to help one another for years to come.

FROM WORKING LIFE TO ILLNESS

During the time that I was working, and the children were young, I also began reading many books related to health. I had just found out about 'hypoglycaemia', the term given to diabetic patients who had low blood sugar and needed to eat. It was the early 80s, and I explained this nervous agitation, which I had been experiencing for years, to my doctor. I said the feeling would improve if I ate something. He very casually said there is no such thing, and it's all in my mind. When I asked about people who are diabetics, all he could say was I may end up as a diabetic.

Fast forward to 1999, I took on a director's job in a large regional area of NSW. I had to travel 80 kilometres one way to work. It was a very busy service which looked after children from babies to six on an occasional care basis. The stress of the job was apparent, plus the travel from home and back. I probably would have stayed longer than the three years I did, because I absolutely loved the people I worked with and remain friends with many of them to this day. When a job came up closer to home that just involved preschool age children and included the school holidays I jumped at the opportunity and applied for the job. In hindsight this was the worse decision I could ever have made. If I thought the last job had elements of stress, boy was I in for a shock. I truly jumped headfirst from the frying pan, straight into the fire.

Just like all the traumas I had experienced in the past I will not go into any personal details. Let's just say that the moment I got the job, having been employed as the director, the person in charge, who makes all the decisions on the programme, and the day to day running of the service, I quickly realized that many directors had come and gone through this service because the unqualified people that were working there liked making the decisions, and controlled a lot of what was going on. I really enjoyed working with the children, and I could tell they benefited so much from the effort I put into group times, stories and songs and the emotional care of each child. It became apparent that even though these other staff members could see I was doing the job I was employed to do, they would make it as hard as possible for me. I was bullied, abused and harassed in that working situation every day, and soon realized I didn't have the coping mechanisms I thought I had. Trauma, upon trauma began stacking into my body as I spent nearly every day worried about how I would be attacked, and sleepless nights trying to analyse and work out how to fix the situation.

My primitive flight/fight mechanism went into overdrive, and in June 2003 I began feeling stinging pain in my body. It started in my left upper arm, like multiple explosions of needles. Within weeks I was feeling needle like sensations in my feet and both arms and hands and then it spread to my torso and neck and face. I had thousands of fine needle like sensations coursing through my body, and not one doctor could work out what it was. December 2003 one neurologist called it fibromyalgia, the name that is given to an illness when you have pain in multiple locations. Whatever medication I was put on it did nothing to relieve the pain. I began losing even more sleep and I began getting more agitated and depressed about my situation. My immune system began breaking down as I started getting many colds, and even asthma, which I had not had since childhood. I spent four nights in hospital on prednisone. I was sick so often I lost all my sick leave and went weeks without being paid.

In 2004 I decided enough was enough. I had to get out of this job, and it was during this time I had reconnected with a dear old friend whom I had trained with as a preschool teacher after leaving high school. She and I, and my husband Robert decided to buy a large house with a garden and convert it into a childcare centre. I left the job at the end of 2004, and we opened our own child- care centre January 2005. The setting up was a mammoth undertaking, but we were very proud of what we had done in a community that had no child- care centre.

It was great having a place of work where I knew I would not be abused or bullied, but of course every business has its stress triggers, and my body couldn't cope with too much more. I kept ploughing through life trying to make something work while at the same time doing whatever I could to relieve the pain I was experiencing. I had already seen many doctors and specialists and natural therapists, and my GP at the time was working her way through any medications that could potentially relieve my pain, but nothing ever did the trick. I worked in our own child-care service two and a half days a week and my partner worked the rest of the week. We both had two full 10 hour working days, plus 5 or 6 hours where we met and discussed important issues about the staff and logistics of running a service with 11 part time staff. It was great having your own business and running things as you wanted, but deep down I knew I was struggling with what was coursing through my body and could not see any solution in sight.

I pushed through life, as I had always done, until one day in February 2006 I went home, and the flood gates burst open. I could not contain my stress/distress any longer. I couldn't stop crying. I began thinking 'is this what it's like to have a nervous breakdown?' Late that night I rang my partner in business. Being the empathetic person, she always was and still is, she suggested I take a break and not come back until I felt better. My partner was taking over the next day, to do her two and a half days, so I was able to let go for a while and try and work out how I was going to get myself past this hump.

It was about this time my doctor had tried every medication she knew of before any heavier drugs, the opioids. After stepping back from work, this is the time I began taking opioids, and I finally got a small amount of pain relief and could sleep a little without waking constantly because of pain. The downside of all of this is that the body gets use to the opioids, and you either increase them or change to another opioid. This began my fourteen-year experience with heavy narcotics for pain, plus all the other myriad of tablets I was put onto as my life just spiralled down into a much darker place than I could ever have imagined.

I never did go back to work after that as I never felt well enough to be able to give the energy needed to look after small children. Not long after that my partner also stepped back and we employed a director, whom we would correspond with regularly.

LIFE GETS EVEN HARDER

It was during the year of 2006 that my mother died, and even though I spent a lot of time with her before she passed, no one is ready to lose their mother and I missed her terribly.

In 2007 I attended my first pain clinic, with high hopes before I left for my three weeks in Sydney. I read the book the experts had written several times and thought about all the things I would learn to deal with the pain. The course was nothing like the book, and I was hugely disappointed by the whole experience. My initial interview with three members of the team was highly confusing. They asked me to tell them about myself. I began talking about the nature of my pain, how I felt like I was getting fried from the inside out, or if someone had put a cattle prod under my skin and was torturing me, and how I felt like I was walking on bits of glass. Well, this all went down like a led balloon. I had no idea that this is not what they wanted to hear and accused me of 'catastrophising'. At that stage I didn't even know what this meant. I even felt like there was something wrong with me that I couldn't get anything out of the course. Many of the others felt the same so I knew in the end it wasn't just me.

Just before attending this pain clinic, I was diagnosed with syringomyelia, which means you have a watery cyst inside your spinal-chord, and mine was from C6 to T10. The specialists and doctors I saw said that this may have something to do with the pain. They really didn't know much about syringomyelia as they had only just begun discovering and trying to study them after MRIs were first invented, which was only about ten years prior to this.

I had my first MRI when they discovered the syrinx inside my spinal cord. I was inside the MRI machine for ninety minutes to complete a full brain/spinal MRI. I closed my eyes and thought about being somewhere else which was peaceful and uplifting, having learnt to do this with the small amount of meditation that I had done. When I came out of the MRI, the operator then said, 'you can now come back, and unfold your arms Mrs Monds'. When I did as I was told, the pain was so intense, as soon as I got up, I passed out with the pain I was experiencing. I was told from then on, not to have an MRI without sedation.

This syrinx or watery cyst was widest at the heart area, so when I experienced what I would call a 'chest attack', which would to many feel like a heart attack, I could virtually do nothing but sit still. I would just sit and cry and often scream with pain as it felt like someone was tightening wire around my chest. The doctor gave me nitro-lingual spray, as if I had angina. Gradually over time I discovered I could get more relief by drinking hot water, as hot as I could manage. I knew when these attacks were about to happen with the strange tightening sensation at the back of my tongue. These chest attacks would go on for the next 14 years. I had my very last chest attack at a friend's place at RV Homebase, which is where I live now, at the end of 2019.

When I came back from the first pain clinic, I found a pain clinic in Bathurst close to where I lived. It was run by a lovely psychologist, who had herself gone through chronic pain. It really was so much better than the first pain clinic. I was taught lots of mindfulness techniques which I still use to this day. This did give me encouragement that solutions do exist outside of the mainstream medical model.

I tried going back to our childcare centre on a Saturday while nobody was there to see if I could cope with having some input into working life again. I would do book work on my own, hoping to work a little. I did this for a while but soon realised that even this was too much. It was a long drive to the childcare centre, almost 70 kilometres one way, and whenever I got home at the end of the day I was totally wiped out.

I DESCEND INTO A DARK SPACE

In 2010 my GP at the time had obviously gone to one of the courses to get patients off opioids. She was determined to take away the one medication which helped relieve a little of the pain for a short period at night. I went home and thought I could do this on my own. The more I tried, the worse it felt, and I was almost too scared to go to the doctor. At one stage she thought she would increase the Lyrica, which is an anti-epileptic drug so then I could go off the pain relief. Her answer was just to double the dose from 300mg to 600mg. The first night I did this I had a psychotic episode and woke up in hospital having missed a whole day. Nothing seemed to make sense.

In the years 2010 and 2011 I had contemplated suicide numerous times. I was on morphine, Lyrica, antidepressants, and many other medications. Nothing seem to make any difference as my whole life was consumed with pain, anxiety and a feeling of being a continual victim of circumstances. It was so consuming, all I wanted to do was escape. I had attended many sessions with groups, psychologists, psychiatrists, and natural healing modalities, but nothing seemed to get me to a stage where something shifted into a phase where I felt any type of healing.

The nightly ritual during this time was to take as much medication as I was permitted to totally bomb me out so I could sleep a little. Robert would rub the soles of my feet as hard as he could to break up the painful crystals. After that Robert would bandage my arms and legs with bandages as tight as I could possibly tolerate, to alleviate the nerve pain close to the surface of my skin. I would lay in bed, close to falling asleep and I could still feel the pain pounding through the bandages. All night my legs would jolt in the bed as the nerves were firing. The doctors called this 'restless leg syndrome'.

During this period, I lost all my teeth, because during a routine x-ray they found I had a major infection at the gum line and eventually it would spread upwards and could kill me. I was getting over the operation and feeling totally miserable, and during this time, on a beautiful April day, Robert had left early to go to a charity dog trial, and I had already written in my journal as to what I needed to do and asked forgiveness of my family for doing such a thing. I got into bed after swallowing about a hundred Kapanole, a morphine- based tablet. Robert got home that night and I was sitting in the recliner. He thought I had fallen asleep in front of the TV. In the morning I woke up at 5.30 and was so totally pissed off because I was still alive. I ran into the bedroom to tell Robert what I had attempted to do. He quickly got me to the hospital. I was in ICU for three days and was then transferred to a mental facility for three weeks. I felt bad because of what I had put my family through. During the three weeks, in a locked facility I saw a psychiatrist many times. They increased my pain relief as well as my anti- depressants. They also found me another doctor and a new pain clinic. This pain clinic was in Orange, and their view on strong pain relief was a little different, although it also changed, in the time I attended the facility. I think the push to solve the 'opioid crises' was high on the agenda in most hospitals.

During this dark period, I never stopped singing. I sang in Finnish and English, and many of the songs spoke to my soul. This was one I sang almost every day, if I could get through it without crying: One Day at a Time by Maryjohn Wilkin & Kris Kristofferson. This song would give me the strength to keep going.

"One day at a time, sweet Jesus. That's all I'm asking from you. Just give the strength to do every day, what I have to do. Yesterday's gone sweet Jesus, and tomorrow may never be mine. Just help me today, show me the way, one day at a time."

Years went by as I again pushed through life. In the year 2012 we shifted closer to Bathurst, hoping that this would improve my life. It merely added to the stress, and in June 2012 I was diagnosed with breast cancer. Robert was with me as the doctor delivered the bad news. He put his arm around me, thinking that I may burst into tears. All I could think was "yippee, this is my ticket out of here". My life didn't feel like a life worth living any longer. It felt a struggle every day just to stay alive and keep being normal. I got the malignant lump removed from my right breast, and the sentinel node removed from under my right armpit. The cancer had already spread. I was scheduled for a second operation and had nineteen nodes removed, and seven of them were cancerous. Chemotherapy and radiation were then scheduled.

The chemotherapy was brutal on my body from the onset. I was scheduled to have six sessions. With the first I ended up, like many others having chemotherapy, vomiting violently for many days after. With the second, I not only vomited and was nauseous, but all the skin peeled off my hands and it was extremely painful. I lathered my hands in goat milk moisturiser, as I was told to, and kept going. On the third chemotherapy session, because I had had reactions to the previous ones, the oncologist said I would be given a milder dose to the two previous ones, a little cousin to the two previous doses. When I got the third dose, I had only received 30mls, and I went into anaphylactic shock, and ended up in emergency because of the severe allergic reaction. That was the end of chemotherapy for me, and at that stage I didn't even care.

Radiation would then begin for five weeks hundreds of kilometres from my home, in Wagga Wagga, so I had to live in an all- purpose built premises for cancer patients. I was lucky because I was not adversely affected by the radiation I received daily under my right arm and even enjoyed myself with the other patients having radiation.

I was also told I would be on a drug called Tamoxifen for ten years. Because of the drug I had continuous hot flushes, and along with the continuous pain I was experiencing, made my life a total misery. The tamoxifen was also stopped after five years, as the oncologist I then had didn't think I needed to have any more discomfort inflicted upon me. I was ever so grateful.

Unfortunately, after the cancer ordeal I was left with very severe lymphedema in my right arm, and that became a problem to be dealt with every day till the present moment. Because 19 nodes were now missing under my armpit, it caused a traffic jam for the lymphatic system. It cannot work properly, and fluid or lymph, builds up all through the limb affected. I had to learn to lymphatically drain my arm twice a day and had to be extremely careful not to get an infection in the right hand or I could easily end up with cellulitis.

Life threatening cellulitis came along five times, and each time if not for Robert recognising the signs of sepsis I would have died. During the earlier stages of the lymphedema, I wore a constrictive sleeve almost constantly, so if cellulitis had already begun developing, no one could see my arm becoming blotchy and red, and as the redness rose higher up my arm, by this stage I didn't have the mental capacity to look under the sleeve and show anyone. Robert recognised the signs of sepsis as I began talking 'ga ga'. I was always rushed to hospital where I would be administered with strong antibiotics for about a week. There was even one episode that was so bad, and the antibiotics were taking so long to kick in, that the doctors were contemplating amputating my arm.

A LIGHT SHINES IN THE DISTANCE

Even though I have headed this 'a light shines in the distance' it was very faint. In my darkest hours I would ask myself, 'what could I do with my life that would bring me some level of joy?' The answer came to me as children's stories came into my head. Because my partner in business and I had run a Rudolf Steiner inspired childcare centre and I had already written many stories for children, from this idea was born the THANKS series, Edition 1, written in 2012 and Edition 2 written in 2014. The acronym stands for "Therapeutic Healing and Nurturing Kids Stories". The stories themselves were healing for me to write, and I really enjoyed doing the illustrations. They are still on Balboa Press web site for sale.

In 2013 we bought our first caravan. Having two daughters who lived two thousand kilometres apart we began travelling between the two. Our first grandchild was also born in 2013, and of course that added great joy to our family. We spent many months in Townsville, Queensland during the winter months, and then as it began to get hotter, we travelled back to Bathurst NSW. It was during this time I also lost my close friend of fifty- three years to cancer, and I still miss her to this day. We are still very much in contact with her husband, who visits us every now and again. Our children have remained friends and that is very special. It was my close friend Pam who gave me the encouragement to write Edition 2 of the THANKS series. All four stories in the book are about coping with depression. Pam worked as a school counsellor, and she kept telling me about all the sad accounts of children and their inability to navigate through the experiences that today's youth must try and cope with. The last story in the book is on suicide, as seen through the eyes of a 'dingo'. Here is the last paragraph of the story:

> *Oh gosh I miss my brother, it's hard to work out why*
> *He's gone away to the world unseen, and I can only cry.*
> *I have the love of others to keep me going on.*
> *Family, friends and many others, I hear his Spirit Song:*
> *"Live your life a happy way" my brother he would say*
> *Even though it was so hard for him, as*
> *The "Black Dog" came his way.*

For three years we travelled up to Queensland where Robert worked on the sugar cane farms. Our dog Ballie travelled with us, and he was my constant companion. It made me walk in the fresh air and helped me to put normality into my life. I had put on a lot of weight. Many of the medications I was prescribed made me extremely hungry, and even though I thought I knew a little about nutrition, I really didn't know what way to turn as far as losing weight.

In 2015 we decided to sell our sixty- five acres just out of Bathurst and just travel. I thought at the time that living in a caravan, in my state of health, would not be too bad. Yes, it was ok for a while, but not having a home to go back to just added to my distress. I really needed a base to go back to even though we loved going back to Townsville, as a second grandchild was born in 2015. This was again a wonderful event in the family, and I tried so hard to be the grandmother I truly wanted to be, but deep down I was aware of the struggle I was experiencing with my health.

WE LOOK FOR A PERMANENT BASE

After doing some travelling back and forwards from NSW to Queensland, and with my health not improving, we began looking for somewhere permanent to live. We felt northern Queensland was too hot and, we wanted to get away from the cold of the central tableland of NSW. In 2017 Robert and I moved to Maryborough Queensland to an over fifties- life- style village. My main aim in doing this was to find a place where Robert could make lots of friends and play as much tennis as he wanted, because that is his passion. I thought along these lines because I sincerely felt that I didn't have long to live. After settling into our new home Robert encouraged me to find a surgeon who would give me a gastric sleeve surgery, hoping it would help with the severe pain condition that wouldn't let up. I had put on enormous weight due to my medications, and sometimes eating poorly because I had lost motivation to try. Six months after moving into the village on the 16th of October 2017 I had the gastric sleeve surgery, and after five weeks nineteen kilos had fallen off. This made me feel good about myself for the first time for years. However, that is where it stopped, and no more of the weight would budge.

Before I go any further, I wish to say that I am in no way giving medical advice to anyone. Each person needs to come to their own conclusion about their own circumstances. I am merely relaying my journey and the steps I took along the way in researching diets and information and making many personal choices about what I would try next. At this stage of the game, I had already been quite entrenched in the mainstream medical model. Doctors had saved my life many times, and for that I was very grateful. However, as my illness had become chronic, and I had already suffered severely for over fourteen years, it became apparent that I needed to begin making other choices if I was to move into any stage of health.

One course I attended to help myself was Tapping The Healer Within. This uses Thought Field Therapy, where you use a sequence of tapping on the face, hands and body to collapse emotions you are experiencing. I still use this quite often to help with any kind of anxiety sleep issues.

It was during this time when I began searching for answers, I was offered an 'Anointing' by a friend, who was also a Christian Minister. I gladly accepted his help and found that I was quite prepared to open my heart and soul to whatever help the universe was offering. Afterall, God works in mysterious ways, and being closed minded was not going to get me anywhere.

MY REAL EDUCATION BEGINS

This is when my real education began in earnest. I had just come into the possession of my first iPad and began researching weight loss diets. Our oldest daughter, Hannele had completed a double degree at La Trobe University in Melbourne, in Nursing and Naturopathy, and she was the first to mention the Ketogenic diet, and that was years prior. I began researching the Ketogenic diet, which was used to help children with epilepsy back in the 1920s before drugs were popular. This was a totally different way of fuelling the body. It also appealed to me because I knew that calorie restriction or starvation diet would be difficult for me and is difficult for most people. The reason for this is that many people have a condition called Insulin Resistance. This has occurred in so many people in today's world because our diets are mainly fuelled by sugars in addition to unhealthy carbohydrates and unhealthy cooking oils. When we have excess glucose in our bloodstream, the body produces large quantities of insulin. Over time our cells are so full of glucose that insulin keeps coming to the cell door, saying "let me in, I have more glucose for you". The cell retaliates and says, "go away I have plenty" and shuts the door. Simplistically, this is what is known as Insulin Resistance. This is the job of insulin, delivering glucose to the cells, an important job in the body. However, the insulin comes up with resistance from the cells because they are already oversupplied with glucose. The insulin then floats around the bloodstream, a dangerous situation leading to Type 2 Diabetes. Because the insulin cannot deliver this glucose the way it is meant to, it then helps the glucose to lay down as fat.

I was insulin resistant for 50 years. Every two or three hours I had to repeat the process of having something to eat because blood sugar spikes and falls, and you are always hungry. I was told by countless doctors "you will end up as a diabetic", but not one doctor or dietician could help turn this around.

THE KETOGENIC DIET

The ketogenic diet consists of 75% Good Fats, 20% Protein, 5% Carbohydrates. This is about 20 to 50 grams of carbohydrates a day. Good fats can be the fat that is in meat, fish, poultry, eggs, dairy (high fat cheese, butter and cream only), and nuts which have a high fat content (macadamias, pecans, and walnuts are the best). Some people on a keto diet include peanuts and cashews, but because I had many health issues, I decided that my diet would be as clean and nutrient dense as I could possibly manage. The amount of carbohydrates varies a lot in seeds and nuts, so I spent a lot of time reading nutritional labels. Protein and fats often go together. Other good fats include avocadoes and avocado oil, olives and olive oil, coconut oil and butter. I also used MCT oil in my hot drinks. This is available in most chemists, and MCT stands for medium chain triglyceride, and is processed by the body for instant fuel. You need to be careful with MCT oil and only start off with a teaspoon. It could easily bring on a quick trip to the toilet.

The only carbohydrates which I included were vegetables, except for potatoes, sweet potatoes, pumpkin and corn. Leafy greens are a must with their high nutrient content and are low in carbohydrates, as well as cruciferous vegetables like broccoli, cabbage and cauliflower, kale and bok choy. Onion and garlic are also important.

Just a final note on oils. I have seen countless You Tube videos on people cooking the most wonderful foods, and then they go and fry their vegetables in canola oil or some other sub- standard seed oil that has found its way onto our grocery shelves. Canola oil is an industrial oil which causes inflammation. I have heard two cases where two different people, having two different independent eye specialists have told them that their macular degeneration can be directly linked to using margarine over years and years, instead of butter. We have been so brainwashed for decades to believe so many lies.

SHOPPING & GETTING STARTED

When I first discovered that I could possibly get my weight loss journey to continue, I was so excited. It is SO important that you educate yourself with the knowledge you need before going out shopping and just buying everything keto. The keto market also contains a lot of processed foods. The people that impressed me on You Tube were those success stories that were the simplest. One of these is 'Butter Bob', and that was what his YouTube channel was called. For breakfast he had bacon and eggs; for lunch he had meat and salad; for dinner he ate steak and vegetables. He used lots of butter, hence the name. If there is no complex medical history, this may also work for others.

You fuel your body with protein and fats, plus have the allowed vegetables, and simply take out the carbohydrates. My case was way too complex, and I had to do much more education and fine tuning to get to a comfortable stage. In fact, I am still doing this to the present day, making changes to make whatever diet I am on, the healthiest I possibly can.

While speaking to many people about fuelling the body with protein and fat, I realised a lot of people were completely convinced that you needed carbohydrates and even sugar to keep the body functioning optimally. Then I found something online that was my big 'ahaa' moment. In the absence of carbohydrates and minimal fat, the body in its infinite wisdom switches on a process call "Gluconeogenesis" and during this process the body uses protein and converts it into glucose for fuel. What a revelation that was. That is why protein needs to be also kept moderate to keep the fat burning process going.

STEPS WHICH I TOOK

1. Eliminate sugar. Then when comfortable

2. Go low carb: 50grams then down to 20grams

3. Take out all grains, such as oatmeal, breakfast cereal, bread, crackers, pasta, biscuits and cakes, pizza and even sour dough. This can be confronting to a lot of people, and believe me I know, as I lived that way for decades and wondered whether I would ever be able to do it. Believe in yourself. Know that inside you is an amazing intelligence that is there for you 24 hours a day and wants only the best outcome for you.

During this time, you will feel hollow and hungry, and that is the time to start eating good quality protein with plenty of good fats. If you let yourself go hungry you will reach for something you shouldn't be having. The style of ketogenic diet I preferred was almost vegetarian, and I prescribed to a vegan You Tube channel called 'Heavenly Fan'. I did have dairy, eggs and fish. Because of the gastric sleeve surgery, I was not able to digest red meat easily. It is very important to keep educating yourself on the style of ketogenic diet you would prefer to be on. That doesn't mean you need to stay with it forever. My diet has changed so many times I have lost count. The significance of learning and making all the decisions yourself about what you eat daily, instead of just being handed a diet to follow, puts the responsibility on YOU. Only in that way will you feel empowered enough to make changes according to your own body's specific needs. Listen to your own body and feel empowered and motivated to make whatever changes you feel necessary.

REPLACING THE OLD FAMILIAR FOODS WITH HEALTHIER OPTIONS

Because I am really interested in the science of food, and how it can be our worst enemy or it can be our medicine, I found lots of recipes on You Tube that replaced the familiar favourites. If you need sweetener in coffee or tea, or for making baked goods, I found the best was stevia or monk fruit which is mostly combined with erythritol. Reading labels is so important. There are many names for sugar, and here are a few: sucrose, fructose, galactose, high fructose corn syrup, and multi-dextrose. All can be researched online. Making cakes was a hard thing to get away from. My mother was a great cook, and I loved baking, and my two daughters are also great cooks. However, I had to begin cooking 'smart', and while on the ketogenic diet I learnt how to make cakes with no sugar, no flour, no butter, although butter was acceptable, I used avocado oil. Bread can also be replaced although this is one food, I found slightly challenging, because the ingredients which you use behave in a totally different manner. Ketogenic ice cream is a great treat and not that hard to make especially if you have an ice cream maker. There are lots of recipes online. The same with delicious biscuits made from almond flour or coconut flour or savoury seed biscuits.

WHY DOES THE KETOGENIC DIET HELP YOU LOSE WEIGHT?

If you do not know the answer to this piece of trivia, you would automatically assume that fat can't help you lose fat. Carbohydrates provides four calories per gram, Fat provides nine calories per gram. That statement alone would make a person fat phobic, but looking at it a little closer, you would not need to eat as many grams of fat to keep you fuelled. In other words, fat will sustain you for longer and will keep you satiated for a longer period. Also, when you eat fat, insulin doesn't really play any lead role in the equation. It is indicated on much of the information I found, that as soon as you begin eating, insulin gets ready to play its part. I have already explained the carbohydrate/insulin connection, and to a lesser degree protein also uses some insulin. Insulin is the fat laying hormone, and the way to trigger it in your body is by consuming anything that has a form of sugar in it. And by that, I mean all forms of sugar: table sugar, fructose corn syrup, honey, and even the healthiest bread on the planet, and I hate to say this but "fruit". During the period of losing weight on a ketogenic diet, I did give 'fruit the boot'. Once I began losing weight on the diet, and yes, I did miss fruit, I would allow myself 20grams of raspberries with cream each day. That was my sweets for about 12 months.

I will now try and explain how the body begins burning its own fat stores. When glucose stores are low in the body, less insulin is floating around because it is not needed as much anymore. However, you have just enjoyed a great steak and eggs and avocado and a healthy leafy green salad. After you finish eating this lovely meal the body is automatically stimulated to produce insulin, but because it's not needed, the body looks at the next preferred fuel source. The protein and fat are often consumed together but let us look at fat first. The body needs fuel for the brain and many other bodily processes for energy. The body begins to burn the fat from the steak, eggs and avocado, and in this amazing process it begins to produce "ketones", hence we get the term ketogenic diet. During this change over period from becoming a carbohydrate burner to becoming a fat burner, is termed becoming 'fat adapted'. You need to consume enough fat so that your body begins to recognise that you are now using fat for fuel. Then when all consumed fat has run out, from the last meal you consumed, the body automatically begins to burn up the fat stores you have in your body. If you do not consume enough fats at the beginning phase, the 'fat adaption' is much harder for the body to recognise. Once this process begins happening daily, that is, fat burning off body fat, then you need to begin tweaking just how much fat to consume in order to get the best results. However, I would suggest not to rush into this part of the process until you feel comfortable with your eating pattern and feel satiated and know you will not crave to cheat.

INTERMITTENT FASTING

After the weight loss began to kick in, I also tried to do some intermittent fasting every day. Intermittent fasting is a strategy that can be used for not only weight loss but also has incredible health benefits. In 2016 a Japanese researcher by the name of Yoshinori Ohsumi was awarded a Nobel Prize for his discovery of a process call Autophagy. This happens in the body when food is taken out of the picture all together. The body turns within, and the cells turn into 'Self-Eating' cells. In other words, the body begins to recycle its own garbage, and can keep itself going during times of self- induced famine. This process can have amazing health benefits and should always be done under a doctor's supervision.

After a while if you can go from dinner, perhaps 8am, and start eating again at 12noon or 1pm, you're eating window gets smaller and you reap the benefits of intermittent fasting. I did this daily for a long time, but because my stomach was so small after the gastric sleeve surgery, I had to be very aware to include high fat foods right up until I went to bed. Even doing this I would still wake up hungry during the night. You do what you can, don't beat yourself up if you can't manage it and just keep chipping away at your goal.

Final note on the ketogenic diet. I used many different doctors' opinions found on You Tube. They didn't all agree with each other, and I feel everyone needs to use their discerning intelligence and take the best out of every bit of information coming their way. Don't forget everything in life is a work in progress. We come across information not in one fell swoop. Very often we need to listen, take it in, use what resonates with you, and be open minded enough to change when your heart leads you in another direction. The You Tube channels I continually went back to: Heavenly Fan; Dr Eric Berg, and typing in the "ketogenic diet" will bring up countless others. I always chose the healthiest options, namely, least amount of processed anything, no sugar and absolutely no bad oils.

EXERCISE

In the winter of 2019, I got up very early one morning and said to myself 'I am going for a walk'. What was I thinking, I hadn't walked very far for years, but something inside me prompted me to begin. The walks got longer and longer and come Christmas I was still walking every day. Of course, it wasn't far, but I kept at it every day despite the pain. I would walk and pray, saying 'thank you God, I thought I would never do this again'. When the warmer weather came, I would of course go for a swim, and that was my enjoyable form of exercise. A pool was built closer to our house and that made it a lot easier. I would also do floor exercises whenever I could manage. Despite years of pain, I could still get onto the floor and was quite flexible. What I wanted to do more than anything in the world was to dance. I could remember what it felt like to dance to rock and rock music, and my heart yearned for that. I also love singing, and I would do that regularly.

By Christmas 2019 I had managed to get to 70 kilograms in weight. Before the gastric sleeve surgery, I weighed 95 kilograms, and I lost 19 kilos immediately after the operation. By Christmas 2019 I had now lost another 4 kilos, and this took two years. It was during that Christmas break that our oldest daughter, Hannele came for Christmas with her family. She was happy for me that I had lost a little bit more weight and could see that I was full steam ahead with this healthy ketogenic diet. I even managed to make a ketogenic cheesecake as part of our Christmas dinner. During the time they were with me I remember my weight went to 69.99 kilos and they would have sworn I had won the lottery, I was so proud of that small shift, and it gave me so much encouragement to just keep going. Hannele could see that I was still very much struggling with the pain which I had then already had for 16 years. She rang me after going home with probably the most important and life changing message I could ever receive. "Mum just look up You Tube and have a look at the work of Dr Joe Dispenza".

DR JOE DISPENZA COMES INTO MY LIFE

I found so much information about this man I don't quite know where to start. I knew he recommended meditation, and all his meditations are on You Tube. There were also many short videos on his explanations of why he teaches this method of meditation. His personal story was miraculous to say the least.

Dr Joe Dispenza had an accident while bicycle racing when he was twenty- three, back in 1986. He crushed six vertebrae and was basically told he would never walk again unless he agreed to have a "Harrington Rod" procedure. He declined this operation to the dismay of many specialist's opinions, and instead discharged himself from the hospital and went and stayed with a good friend. From this point he began speaking to the 'loving intelligence' that he believes lives within you and all around you. He put lots of focused attention and intention to the inside of his body, telling this intelligence what he wanted to achieve. He visualised in his meditation for many hours per day about what the vertebrae needed to look and change back to. Being a trained chiropractor, the visualisation part was relatively easy. After putting in many weeks of work doing this form of meditation every day, he was back on a bike within twelve weeks. What a miracle.

When I told Hannele that I loved Dr Joe Dispenza meditations and I would keep doing them for as long as I need to, she decided to buy me my first two Dr Joe Dispenza books:

BREAKING THE HABIT OF BEING YOURSELF and

BECOMING SUPERNATURAL

I have read them both, and they outline everything you need to do. The important element of this type of meditation is that you understand the formula to create healing, and by reading the books, and absorbing the wonderfully written and researched information, you can assign meaning to what you do when you close your eyes to meditate. These meditations are in no way passive. You must work hard mentally.

I began with BREAKING THE HABIT OF BEING YOURSELF, as I quickly realized I needed to come out of that victim consciousness that I had put myself into through all my own thoughts, feelings, emotions, words, actions and experiences. I had carried all the memories of these thoughts and emotions with me for years, reaffirming to myself repeatedly that this is what made me sick. I began to realize that doing just that alone kept me stuck in a continual loop of addiction to my own unhealthy thoughts, that generated the emotions of the past traumas repeatedly. Dr Joe explains this loop, with our thinking and feeling. You feel the way you think, and you think the way you feel. Whatever way this is for an individual, is the path that your destiny is aligned to. I was thinking as a victim, and I felt victimised in life. I soon realised I desperately needed to break those emotional bonds, which were tying me to the past and I wasn't getting past the trauma of my past experiences. I won't say that this was easy. Because the original 2003 PTSD incident was etched in my brain, and the pain I felt continually reaffirmed these emotions, I would keep re-experiencing this same level of trauma, multiple times a day for over a decade. This happened automatically through thought alone. I was in a constant state of vigilance, expecting the worst from everything around me. I now know that from that original moment of trauma, I stopped evolving as a human being, and the ability to be present with family and friends in the moment was always difficult, because all my energy was consumed by living in a state of survival. Even the smallest things would trigger the PTSD thoughts, and any small thought would trigger the feelings of pain and panic that became my state of being. I was so unaware of the damage I was allowing to escalate inside my body. I had conditioned my body into being addicted to the past, not consciously, but through the emotions of the past, which I had boxed up and kept as some sort of unwanted gift within my sub-conscious mind.

After reading BREAKING THE HABIT OF BEING YOURSELF, I can honestly say, it was very confronting to expose and really look at what I had been creating for decades, but I just persevered. When I began, I could barely sit up to meditate for any length of time, but gradually as things shifted, and I improved, I had no problem. For more than a year I could never meditate in the morning because I always woke up with anxiety. I chose to meditate after lunch and then just before going to sleep.

Breaking the emotional bonds of the past, means also forgiving everyone from your past. That does not mean that you forget what traumas you went through and the people that were involved. It means letting go emotionally. When you can think of the traumatic incident you went through, and there is no emotional charge, this is the time in your life you have gained wisdom from your experiences. Forgiveness is not denying you went through the experience or saying that it was OK. By forgiving you release yourself from the damage that emotion can do to your body.

Through all this healing of trauma, pain, guilt, shame, and unworthiness, I realised I had to begin 'loving myself' and respecting my own boundaries like I had never done before. I looked at how I let this develop, and realised I needed to forgive myself first and foremost. After that I could see myself as being worthy of healing on every level. I never knew how important it was to learn to love myself, in order to feel worthy enough to receive. I now sense that loving space around me, through meditation. Dr Joe Dispenza says often, "Love Heals All". Love is in the top highest frequencies of energy. When I am truly connected to the 'Void', that loving intelligence, that intelligent love, I now know what this frequency of love feels like in your body as you meditate. It is such a wonderful blissful feeling; it makes you never want to stop the practice of meditation. I also came to realise, the more I can open my heart, to love, compassion, kindness and gratitude, my Reiki also becomes stronger.

When Dr Joe Dispenza said, "now find a new future", that was literally the hardest thing for me to do as all I could see in the future was more pain, suffering and death. What my visualization consisted of for me was myself dressed in a beautiful ballet dress and dancing on the grass to beautiful music. The music I chose came from You Tube, called Spirit Tribe Awakening, Self- Love Healing, 432Hz Music for Meditation, Ancient Frequency Music. This beautiful music I chose was very healing, and I did this meditation/visualization every day for over a year. I still listen to it very frequently, bringing back all the memories of self-healing in the last two and half years. When a fancy- dress party came up in the village we live in, I knew I had to dress up as a fairy in a ballet dress. This was twenty months after beginning the Joe Dispenza meditations every day. I had such a great time at that fancy dress party. I danced all night and was in a state of complete joy as I danced with my friends. I had literally walked into my New Future.

I have heard Dr Joe Dispenza say many times, thoughts and feelings and emotions all work together. Thoughts are the language of the brain, and feelings are the language of the body. Put strong emotions with it, whether positive or negative, and the thoughts and feelings are accentuated. Within six months of beginning Dr Joe's meditations, I knew that something inside me was shifting. I wasn't out of pain by any means, but I did feel confident enough in July 2020 to say to my doctor, "I am going to come off all of these medications". I had been on strong opioids for fourteen years, and on Remembrance Day, 11/11/ 2020 I took my last opioid. I had already taken myself off anti-depressants, anti-psychotics, anti-inflammatories, anti-biotics and the sleep medication which caused injury to my face, as I would get up to go to the bathroom, fall asleep on the toilet and fall on the tiled floor. (See Visuals April 2018). Word of warning I am in no way suggesting, for anyone to come off their prescription medication. My doctor was aware of what I was doing, and he was supportive.

By this time, November 2020 I had lost in total 35 kilograms. I could walk better, had more energy and was feeling happier. After going off all the medication, I realised that I got my consciousness back, but the pain had not quite gone away. That took me back to the iPad for more research. This coincided with a particular time in our lives when Robert was facing his own health issues. How could we improve our diet, so we could have optimal health? We were floundering because we always assumed we ate so well and had no reason to doubt what had been mainstream for such a long time. After all Robert came from a dairy farm and I grew up on a poultry farm. All our married life we had lived on sheep and cattle farms which Robert managed.

Very close to this period we also went to see an Integrative Doctor. This is a doctor trained in the normal medical way, as well as being trained to see the body as a whole and look outside of the mainstream medical model. In the US an integrative doctor is a doctor of functional medicine, and they are very much interested in all aspects of the patient's health including diet, lifestyle, how much stress you are under and whether you are getting all your minerals and vitamins. After going to the integrative doctor, we began alkalizing our body every day and were very aware of acid and alkaline forming foods. The integrative doctor also wrote on his notes for us, to look up the work of Dr Max Gerson, who pioneered the Gerson Therapy, and documented excellent results for cancer and other diseases in "Healing the Gerson Way". I took some of this on board and had a profound 'healing crisis' which took me another step further down my healing path.

We also did a great deal of research on- line. This led us down a path we would not have even imagined in our wildest dreams. We came across a doctor and researcher by the name of Professor T. Colin Campbell, who also grew up on dairy farm, and he was involved in researching the effects of animal protein on human health. T. Colin Campbell is the researcher and author of "The China Study". If you are interested you can find him on You Tube, either under his name or Whole Food Plant Based Diet. He coined the term, and this is the diet we thought we should try.

I was keen to start this diet as soon as I found out about making another positive change. I had for the last few weeks began noticing many lumps under my left arm and through my breasts. It was painful to lift my left arm, and I thought that the breast cancer was returning. I had tried massaging under my arm, but the lumps remained.

It was stressful becoming a vegan cook overnight. The diet was not only whole food plant based, and had to be healthy, I was very conscious of making it as tasty as possible, so we could make it sustainable. I persevered and kept going, and to my great delight and surprise, the pain left my body after one month on this diet. I was also meditating daily, and these results put me into a state of bliss. I was ecstatic as I was pain free for the first time in 17 years.

When something like this happens to you, as Dr Joe says, the body takes a snap- shot of exactly what you were doing at that time. I know I was meditating twice a day and eating only plants. It was like having a fire within your body for seventeen years, and the fire suddenly was extinguished. The inflammation at the end of December 2020 was gone, and the gratitude I felt was so overwhelming I would cry with happiness. Six weeks after beginning the whole food plant-based diet, my breasts became soft, and all the lumps disappeared under my left arm. Another bonus came along with this as well. I shed another five kilos. In total I had now lost forty kilograms, 42% of my body weight.

WHOLE FOOD PLANT BASED DIET

Once I went onto this way of eating, I never looked back. I still meditate twice a day and stick to mainly a whole food vegan diet. I was very strict for 19 months, after which I occasionally would have eggs and a little fish. The intense chronic pain has not returned, but experience has made me very mindful as to what I put into my mouth. This way of eating will not be popular with everyone because a lot of our familiar everyday foods are not included, and the healthiest option on this diet is very labour intensive. At this stage I didn't even care because the results I was experiencing within my own body with the changes I had made to my life were worth every bit of effort I had already put in in the past year.

Once I got my head around how to prepare this type of food and feel the health benefits of my whole daily routine, I began to relax with the whole thing. Now I stick to preparing the foods we really enjoy eating, and occasionally I'll go to greater efforts, such as preparing Finnish flat bread, called "Rieska", which can be used for pizza crust, as well as wraps. I always make it with healthy ingredients, so this is not the genuine Finnish way of making it. Here is my recipe:

- 1 cup cooked mashed sweet potato/potato/pumpkin or any one or combination of these
- 1 to 2 cups wholemeal spelt/buckwheat/millet/barley or any good organic flour. This is an approximate.
- 1 teaspoon salt, 1 flat teaspoon bicarb soda (optional)

I also added this to help bind the ingredients when dealing with thin pastry: 1 tablespoon of ground flax seed meal with 3 tablespoons of boiling water, wait awhile until it becomes gelatinous and add to the mix All of these are combined in a bowl. Mix until you need to use your hands to bring it together to form a dough ball. Keep adding the flour until you feel it is pliable enough to work on and roll out on a floured surface. I bake the pizza crust before adding delicious ingredients on top. With the wraps I roll out thin small portions and fry with a little good quality oil, brown on both sides and cool on a plate.

The YouTube channels which I use for the Whole Food Plant Based Diet: Forks over Knives, The Whole Food Plant Based Cooking Show, Plant Based Science London, The Physician's Committee, and Eating with Plants.

The choice of diet for each person is individual. No one person is the same as another. During our extensive research into the optimal diet for health, particularly when it comes to heart disease and cancer, a lot of the research did NOT recommend high levels of animal protein and fat, as cancer cells can feed off many sources, the main ones being sugar, fat and animal protein. The research mainly comes from the experience, research and books written by: Jane McLelland "How to Starve Cancer Without Starving Yourself", who cured herself of stage 4 cancer three times; "Fight Prostate Cancer and Win" by Ron Gellatley; Professor T. Collin Campbell "The China Study"; Thomas Campbell MD "The Campbell Plan". Whatever diet you choose for yourself must be satiating and sustainable over the long term. Above everything you must believe in yourself and be prepared to look outside of the square. Also be prepared to take a different fork in the road, if your discerning intelligence is telling you to do just that. Make changes as YOU see necessary and monitor the changes.

After beginning to eat this way, plus spending hours of the day meditating, many people began to ask me – 'well how did you do it?' When I began to tell them about the effort I had to put into getting into a better state of health, such as the labour-intensive diet that required a lot of preparation and the time spent meditating, I often got this reply- 'wow I could never do that'. The only reply I could ever come back to them with: 'well my incentive was MASSIVE'.

> *"Your Diet is only as good as the Health that you Feel."*

As I spoke to my daughter, Hannele who recommended Dr Joe Dispenza, I mentioned that my pain had virtually gone. I just had gotten over at least a decade of restless leg syndrome, where my legs would jolt involuntarily as I slept, and the nerves were constantly fired up and hurting night and day. The integrative doctor had put me onto magnesium glycinate, and after taking that for about four weeks the restless leg syndrome subsided. I said to Hannele "I still have frozen legs from the knees down" and I would have to always wear socks at night. Hannele just laughed and said to me "Mum just keep meditating and doing exactly what you are doing. You have healed yourself of seventeen years of very severe chronic pain. I'm sure you will also heal these frozen legs." Her confidence in me doing this form of healing meant so much to me and I knew that I needed to do just that. My meditations just got better and better. I have had some amazing mystical experiences. I rang her three weeks later and said that the frozen legs had reduced itself to the ankles and it was just my feet now. She laughed again and said, "it won't be long, and you will ring and tell me that it's all gone." Two weeks later I did just that. Hannele was overjoyed for the progress that I had made. I was truly learning to let go of so much. The words I used kept coming up each time I meditated: 'Trust, Surrender, Let Go, Let God'

> *"If you want to find the secrets of the universe,*
> *Think in terms of energy, frequency and vibration"*
> Nikola Tesla

Hannele also gifted me with two more Dr Joe Dispenza books YOU ARE THE PLACEBO & EVOLVE YOUR BRAIN

When Christmas rolled around 2021, she also gifted me the best gift I could get from her: Dr Joe Dispenza's Online Progressive Intensive. I loved every minute of it. Hannele also bought the course for herself, and we decided together that we would attend a Week- Long Retreat as soon as Joe Dispenza comes to Australia once more. I am looking forward to that event very much, but leading up to it, I will just keep plugging away at meditating every day.

The Joe Dispenza meditations that I have used the most are: "Tuning into New Potentials"; "Blessing of the Energy Centres";" Pineal Breathing Meditation"; "You are the Placebo"; "Water Rising"; "Heart/Brain Coherence"; "Changing Boxes". These are not in the order I began, and there are many more. I followed what was in the book I started with, BREAKING THE HABIT OF BEING YOURSELF, then I began to work through others. I also used meditations from other meditation teachers, Sarita Sol, as well as Jess Shepherd. There are plenty to choose from, but if you are just beginning your meditation journey, I suggest short meditations to begin with, and keeping it simple, so you don't lose interest.

As I write this, it is mid May 2022, and I need to speak about some of the wonderful experiences I have had in the meditations I do. For over two months now my nightly ritual is the meditation called "The Generous Present Moment". It puts me into such a wonderful headspace to go to sleep. For many years I slept very poorly. Even now I still wake up every hour or two to go to the toilet, but at least I go to sleep in between. For many years I spent countless nights with no sleep at all, so every bit of progress I make, I am extremely grateful.

There have been other well- known writers and speakers who have impacted my healing journey. BRUCE LIPTON Ph.D. is one of those special people. Hannele also gave me the book by Bruce Lipton call THE BIOLOGY OF BELIEF. The book itself is amazing as he goes into the science of cells and how they behave depending upon the environment they are subjected to. It was thought for a long time that our genes signal the environment, which creates disease and illness. Through Bruce Lipton's research into EPIGENETICS, it has become apparent that it is the environment which signals the gene. He says that genes do not have an on/off mechanism, and only 1% of genes are connected to disease. However, depending upon the environment which these genes are bathed in, they have the potential to upgrade for health or down grade for disease.

The mechanism that turns the environment on is the BRAIN. What we think, and how we feel about the pictures we see in our mind translates into complementary medicine. Consciousness changes the chemistry in our brain, as our body chemistry complements the consciousness. Whatever chemical cocktail you are producing, this controls your genetics and behaviour. For example, when you are in love you are in pleasure, and you glow. Your body is releasing love hormones dopamine, oxytocin, vasopressin, as well as growth hormone.

The BRAIN is the architect, which alters the 'read-out' of the genes through the proteins it signals, from what you think and feel, your consciousness. We create disease with our consciousness. Many people stay in victim consciousness for years like I did, hooked on being a victim, with guilt, shame, resentment and fear. Your mind can alter the blueprint, depending on the protein that is activated from how you see the world. We are all powerful architects of our future.

Another significant influence on my healing journey has been GREGG BRADEN, Hannele also giving me two of his outstanding books: THE SPONTANEOUS HEALING OF BELIEF and THE WISDOM CODES. The later has wonderful healing words, 'ancient words to rewire our brains and heal our hearts'. I have listened to a lot of Gregg Braden on You Tube. One I loved was on the 'Lost Gospel of St Thomas', and the art of prayer.

"Mind is the Matrix of all Matter" - *Max Planck Physicist*

2022 IS HERE NOW

We have now lived in this over- fifty's life- style village for five years. I feel so much has happened in those five years. In the beginning I was a totally different person to who I am today. I found it hard to talk and socialize with people as I could feel energies from everyone around me. I usually lasted about an hour in any social situation. I would take myself home, lay down and was exhausted. I socialise and talk to many more people now and I can last longer in any social situation. Whenever there is dancing in the village, I love attending and I make the most of the time I have there. We have some wonderful entertainers in the village and their singing creates a lot of joy for many of us.

My health is at a great level. This is the best I have felt for two decades. For a person that was fainting at least once a week, I have now not lost consciousness for over two years. So much has changed. It was as if I woke up from the worst nightmare of my life, which lasted seventeen years, and emerged into waking human life just as the covid 19 pandemic had started.

Just the whole world- wide pandemic, pushed me into becoming a stronger person, not just physically and health wise, but also to know how to honour my own decision- making ability. During the years of taking so many medications, my body became allergic to a long list of drugs, which I need to keep on my health records. It was early 2020 when, out of the blue, I received a phone call from my oncologist in NSW. He was ringing to warn me about the covid vaccine. In 2012 when I was having chemotherapy and I had experienced an anaphylactic reaction, there were two ingredients which he said I was highly allergic to, and both ingredients were in the covid 19 vaccine. I thanked him as I was extremely thankful for the information. When I asked for this in writing, he refused and told me to go to my GP who would send me to an immunologist. I had the names of the two ingredients on my phone, Docetaxel and Paclitaxel, and I gave them to the GP, but he told me he couldn't put anything in writing because he could lose his licence. I was, at this stage, getting quite frustrated, as everyone around me was getting immunised, and I felt I had valid reasons for an exemption to the vaccine.

I rang up Daffodil Cottage in Bathurst, where I had the chemotherapy, and asked for my records on that anaphylaxis incident to be sent to me. Once I had that in front of me, and it stated in bold print: **severe allergic reaction**, I felt I had the evidence and was confident to go ahead with an appointment with the immunologist. By this stage my GP and the immunologist had a copy of the report, and I felt there would not be any issues to resolve. Boy was I wrong.

The phone appointment with the immunologist proceeded like this: 'yes, I can see what you are allergic to, and yes, those ingredients are in both of our vaccines'. I then asked: 'so I will get an exemption?'. The answer was 'No No, we are not into the business of giving exemptions. We would like you to come to Royal Brisbane and Women's Hospital, so we can immunise you'. I was stunned, and in my stupor, I said 'but I'm allergic to the ingredients'. The answer I got back made me feel that the whole world had gone mad. This is what she said: 'Because this is such a safe environment and both vaccines are so safe, we would like you to come into the hospital, we will vaccinate you. If something happens, we can bring you back to life, and then you won't have to have a second one'. This whole thing left me feeling somewhat uneasy about the mainstream medical arena.

On a positive note, 2022 has also brought new friends into my life. I have been blessed to meet a small group of spiritually minded people in the village I live in. It's a very small group, and we discuss so many different topics of common interest, plus the group enjoy doing some of my meditations. The meditations I write are very much inspired by Dr Joe Dispenza, as I have gained so much from this man.

One of the members, Vivienne, introduced us all to Qi Gong, and we all love doing that small exercise routine together. Another exercise, a Tahiti Yoga pose, which I call 'Legs Up', was also introduced into the group by Vivienne. I was very interested as this was an exercise that would reset your autonomic nervous system. This involves laying on the floor, preferably on a soft mat, with no pillow, and you put your legs on a lounge or if you are short like me, on a smaller stool with pillows to the height so your legs are resting at right angles, or you can have your legs going straight up if can tolerate this. You need to do this for 14 days straight, at the same time, no talking, or listening to any device. The aim is to completely chill out for half an hour. If you have any interruptions in that half hour, like having to get up to do something, you need to begin the 14 days all over again. After the 14 days you can then just do this whenever you feel the need. I chose to include this in my daily routine as soon as I wake up. I have everything set up near my bed. I can say, in all honesty, this helps calm down your nervous system. Because I have given my autonomic nervous system such a whipping over the years, I took this on board in a big way. I have gone way past the 14th day, but it has certainly lowered a lot of anxiety within me.

This technique can be found on the livingfreemovement.org website. There is some general information, then to access further information, it is by subscription, $100 for each of the platforms for a year. The video I saw at Vivienne's place, refers to this Autonomic Nervous System reset, and is on the Heal Me platform. On this platform, search #1 Live Long and Prosper series. The relevant part of this video is at 38 minutes 50 seconds. It only goes for a few minutes.

Early in 2022, I went to the optometrist to have my eyes checked and get prescription sunglasses. After doing all the routine tests on my eyes, I could see her looking from one computer screen to another. She looked perplexed and puzzled. I asked what was wrong, was there a problem she had found? She shook her head, and said that there wasn't a problem, but she was confused. The reason for this she explained were the two comparison screens. One was from the year 2019, the other from 2022. I had a 10% improvement with my vision in three years, and a 20% improvement with the inner health of my eye. She explained that the condition which I have, called Retinoschisis, which involves the layers in the inner eye separating, and causing danger to your vision. Back in 2019, the top layer was extremely thin, and they were worried it would break. On this day, in February 2022, the top layer showed an increase in thickness of 20% from three years ago. The optometrist said she had never seen this before, and was puzzled how someone could reverse this condition, and even more rare for someone in their late 60s. I was overjoyed, to say the least, and I knew all my hard work was paying off.

In 2022 my meditations took on another level. Dr Joe Dispenza explains that if you have lived for years in that state of fight/flight, the amount of adrenalin you produce must go somewhere. Very often it is stuck in your limbs or other parts of the body somewhere and, needs releasing. Towards the end of

January 2022, I began to experience physical sensations. These experiences range from feeling electricity very strongly in my body, particularly on the crown of my head, to actual shakings of my limbs and torso. Since these experiences began, they have just continued. Each night as I go into my favourite Dr Joe Dispenza meditation, called the 'Generous Present Moment', I always get some shakings and always feel sparks around my body. I have also experienced seeing fractal patterns four times now, and I find that experience quite uplifting and very mystical. What I see are beautiful geometric shapes, with all the colours of the rainbow inside them, and they move and swirl around the periphery of my direct vision. Sometimes the experience lasts up to fifteen minutes.

CONCLUSION

My life has become a quest for health and wellbeing. So much of my day is spent thinking about which meditation I will do after lunch, what foods I will prepare today, and then a lot of time is spent cutting up fresh vegetables. I still eat a very healthy whole food plant-based diet with a little egg and fish. I still research the Whole Food Plant Based Diet and recipes from a wide variety of sources. I like to go for a walk every day, do a small exercise routine on the floor which helps keep me supple, as well as Qi Gong, and stretches for the whole body.

This may sound strange, but I spend a lot of time in my head, being conscious of not becoming unconscious about my thoughts and feelings. I use many I AM statements, such as 'I am full of joy' 'I am in love with life' I am in an optimal state of health'. This may sound like I will fake it till I make it, but when you realise that unhealthy feelings can be generated in the body through thought alone, then it really doesn't sound too ridiculous at all. What we think and how we feel about the pictures we see in our mind, directly influences the proteins and chemistry generated by the body. Consciousness changes the chemistry in our brain and and is the leading factor in gene expression, through the proteins it signals in the body.

When I was telling my good friend Christine, who lives in Bathurst, of the intensive routine I have taken on during my day and how much of my time is spent caring for 'me', she laughed and said to me: "Don't worry, that isn't being selfish. You call that *high maintenance.*" She certainly is right about that, but I know now, that I will not give up on myself.

I have continued to do Reiki every day, even when I was extremely unwell, I could still feel the electrical sensation in my hands. Throughout this process of healing, the Reiki has only got stronger, and fits very well into my practice of meditation and prayer. I say prayer because I have always been a person who believes in God. Now God has taken on a whole new meaning for me, as I believe this Divine energy lives within me and all around me. The physical sensations I experience in my body during meditation is electro-magnetic. The more I open my heart and feel love, joy and kindness, the stronger the sensation becomes. We all have access to Source, the Creator, and we all part-take, either consciously or unconsciously in co-creating our reality. This Intelligence is Omnipresent and is not just able to be accessed by special people in high places. It is there for everyone; we are all equal. Your INTENTION is the most significant ingredient in this equation. This is all linked to the power of consciousness, a subject I am very interested in pursuing in greater depth.

We all have the power to heal. We deserve to live life and enjoy being here. I know the last time I saw my two grandchildren who live in Townsville, it was so wonderful to enjoy their company. It was the first time in their lives that I have been well enough to be a real grandmother who is happy and wants to be in their company. That alone gives you such a warm feeling in your heart. Now our youngest daughter has given birth to her first child, and we are so looking forward to meeting and holding her in our arms. Five years ago, I thought I would never see these events unfold, let alone be so well that I could experience this level of joy in my life ever again.

Now two and half years after starting this self-healing journey, I still meditate twice a day, I eat a very healthy, mainly whole food plant-based diet, with some eggs and a little fish. I do get a bad back occasionally, and I do not have the stamina of many people my age or even older. I have some sleep issues, and daily I still consciously heal my anxiety problems. My journey towards health and wellbeing will probably be a lifelong goal. Whatever comes along in the future, I will use the skills I have learnt in the last two and half years, plus I will acquire more skills in the future ahead of me, however long I have left on this earthly plane. I cannot see what lies in my future. I only know I will attempt to live every day from a conscious and loving reality.

Meditation has become a cornerstone to my being able to let go of all the daily events and go into the 'void', which gives you such peace before you fall asleep. Dr Joe Dispenza's meditation called, "The Generous Present Moment" has become my nightly ritual, and a great way to let go of the day. When you truly let go of your body, your environment and time, your whole body feels so close to that wonderful loving intelligence that lives within you and all around you. I feel incredible gratitude to Dr Joe Dispenza, and the profound body of knowledge and wisdom he has given to humanity.

It is my wish to impart as much as I can, of what I have gone through and experienced to reclaim back my health. I was told so often to stop searching and accept the fact that I would be in a state of chronic pain forever. I am so grateful, my inner voice won out. I have always been open to all new ideas and modalities. In 2020 I literally woke up from a 17-year nightmare, with a relentless drive to seek out more health intervention than what was being presented to me.

This became an over-riding force that led me to keep searching and learning everything I could. Now in 2022, after many years of insurmountable struggle and pain, and then emerging into a life of happiness and wellbeing, I can only now admit:

My Life's Greatest Adversity has led to my Greatest Awakening.

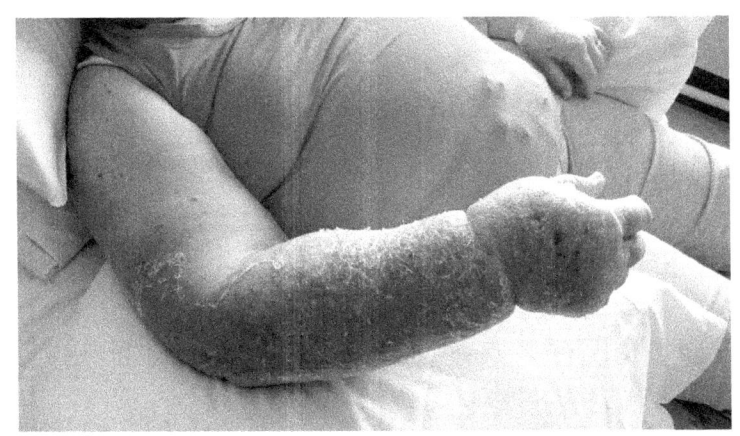

January 2017

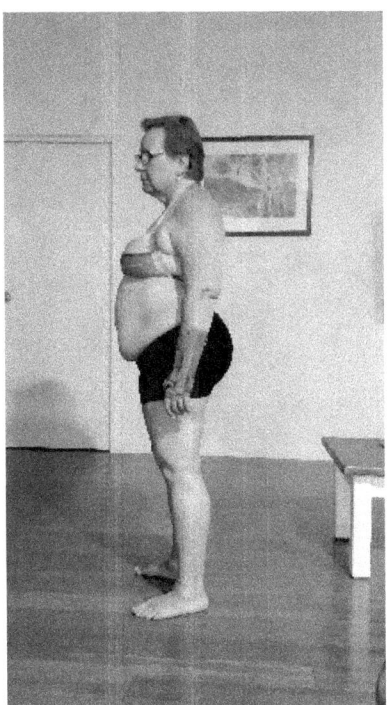

October 2017

October 2017

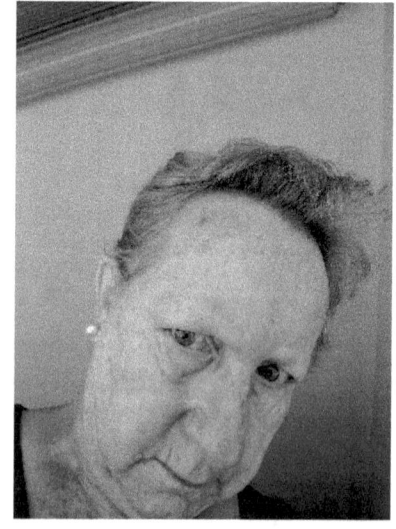
April 2018

May 2019

August 2021

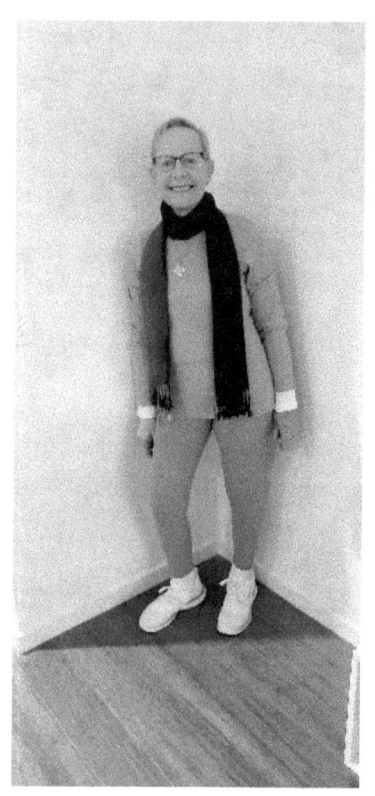

July 2022

*"Everyone has a doctor in him or her;
we just have to help it in its work.
The natural healing force within each of
us is the greatest force in getting well."*
                                    -Hippocrates

My name is Pirkko Monds. I am a Finnish born Australian, living in Maryborough, Queensland with my husband Robert. I am a retired Early Childhood and Primary school teacher. My career was cut short because of severe illness. This is my story of how illness manifested in my body, the chronic pain I endured for 17 years, and the steps I took to come through this long illness. In 2020 I began a self-healing journey that led me, not only to a life of health and wellbeing, but also down many learning paths which opened my mind and heart to embrace many alternate avenues of healing. I lost 40 kilograms during this time, beginning with surgery and then learning how to prepare both ketogenic and plant-based food. I also learnt how to meditate and bring a sense of peace into my life. After two decades I now am at a stage in life when I can enjoy being alive once more, and I am thankful every day for the life altering journey that has led me to this point.

www.ingramcontent.com/pod-product-compliance
Lightning Source LLC
Chambersburg PA
CBHW070327120526
44590CB00017B/2830